SWEDISH CULINARY CLASSICS
RECIPES WITH HISTORY AND ORIGINALITY
CARL JAN GRANQVIST LENA KATARINA SWANBERG

Flavors from the forest and the sea

In Sweden, summertime is closely associated with sensuality and enjoyment, especially when it comes to eating. This is not so strange. Sweden is located really far up in northern Europe. Essentially only several decades ago, fresh food was available only during the relatively short, sunny, warm part of the year. Only in summertime can you eat outside in the garden, organize a picnic or gather for a coffee party on the glassed-in veranda.

Meals in spring and early summer remain a joyous tribute to Swedish Ôrst harvest produce. The year's Ôrst grilled perch, rolled Baltic herring Ôlets that turn into a dill-fragrant casserole when baked in the oven, fresh green asparagus, the Ôrst Swedish strawberries from the outdoor market. Or new potatoes boiled with dill, carried steaming hot to the table and eaten with butter … All pure enjoyment.

The Swedish culinary tradition is otherwise very much a culture of food storage. During the brief summer harvest period, people mainly gathered what they needed and saved it for future use. The long, dark period of the year was always waiting around the corner. People would have to survive then on the bounty of summer. Eating fresh berries was a Öeeting luxury, since most berries were cooked into jam for winter. Eating fresh vegetables was almost wasteful, since vegetables needed to be preserved or pickled. The same was true of potatoes and other root vegetables, which were stored in an earth cellar and served as winter food. The fruits that were available in winter were considered more precious than summer apples and August pears, no matter how delicious.

Swedish bread was traditionally also baked with a long shelf life in mind. Rye bread was baked slowly into durable dark *kavring* loaves or dried into crispbread (*knäckebröd*) or rusks (*skorpor*) that could be stored for long periods. Fresh bread was a luxury for the few. Was it actually so nutritious? In any event, old bread was supposed to be eaten Ôrst.

Similarly, drinking fresh milk or eating fresh butter and eggs was a pleasure when it occurred. Butter and eggs were ordinarily meant to be sold. Milk was fermented or otherwise preserved with the aid of bacterial cultures, becoming various yoghurt-like soured milks (including *filmjölk* and stringy *långfil*), curdled milk (*filbunke*) or sour cream (*gräddfil*). Or else it was made into cheese.

A traditional Swedish housewife's main source of pride was always having a well-Ôlled pantry in preparation for winter. It was a matter of honor that no one had to leave the table hungry. Those who did not eat everything offered to them were made to feel ashamed. In the 18th century the mother of all Swedish cookbook authors, Cajsa Warg, used a motto that, for centuries, summed up the Swedish approach to cooking and enjoying food: "You take what you have."

From a combination of severe winter climate and intensive summer light, Swedish home cooking was born. It is loaded with culinary delights. A wide variety of fresh Swedish ingredients are available – including seafood, poultry, lamb, beef, veal and wild game. Traditional methods of smoking, fermenting, salting, drying, marinating and poaching continue to create their own taste sensations. Open and cultivated landscapes extend from northern to southern Sweden, but so do deep forests. Forests and wetlands not only provide wild game but also mushrooms, lingonberries, blueberries and cloudberries. Those who spend their summers picking and drying juniper berries, bog-myrtle and various home-grown herbs have no problem at all in seasoning and varying the Öavors of warm, hearty winter stews. On the contrary, Swedish home cooking is both Ôlling and tasty.

But what about reÔnement? Elegance? Are there any storage methods mainly intended to create more subtle and delicate taste sensations? Well, for many years the Swedes had a habit of borrowing such luxuries from other culinary cultures, especially that of France, a country where people know the art of living in order to eat. Swedish culinary tradition is instead based on people's need to eat in order to live. They often let their food stop them from talking.

It is thus all the more exciting that today's young generation of Swedish chefs has scored major successes abroad with their tasty creations, which are innovative in both color and design. Modern chefs use lingonberries, cloudberries, root vegetables, Baltic herring, wild game and

not least Västerbotten cheese in new ways, but they continue to be inspired by the richness of centuries-old Swedish culinary traditions. In this way, tastes inspired by the country's vast forests, numerous lakes and long seacoast live on – both in more sophisticated settings and in everyday Swedish life. The dishes presented here are examples of well-prepared Swedish home cooking – classics that grace family tables and in some cases are also found on that world-famous Swedish buffet table known as the *smörgåsbord*.

In sharp contrast to the country's mainly needs-focused meal tradition are the pastries and desserts featured at Swedish coffee parties. Soft, sweet yeast bread made with saffron, butter, sugar, raisins and cinnamon. Almond paste Ôlling. Seven kinds of cookies. Meringues, curd cakes, apple

pies, vanilla sauces and pastries so overÖowing with jam, cream and chocolate that no one has seen anything like them.

Nowadays cinnamon buns are baked all over the world, but to experience a genuine Swedish "cake table" the best suggestion is to travel to the countryside. There, no one lets their food stop them from talking. Year round, your hosts will insist that you sample a little of everything. The conversation Öows, people sing songs together and they gorge on tasty desserts and pastries. Take an extra look at that genuine Swedish princess cake pictured on page 45 – swelling with whipped cream, sponge cake and jam, all swept inside a light green marzipan exterior, powdered with confectioner's sugar. A pink rose crowns its top.

This is how the Swedish love of eating deÔes the long winter: with warm food inside, and summer colors topping the cake.

Enjoy your meal! Or as we say in Swedish: *Smaklig måltid!*

Preparation

Finely dice the onion and sauté gently in a little butter without browning. Soak the breadcrumbs in milk. Blend the ground meat, preferably in a food processor, with the onion, egg, milk/bread-crumb mixture and the spices to the proper consistency and taste. Add a little water if the mixture feels too firm. Check the taste by test-frying one meatball. Then shape small meatballs with the aid of two spoons and place on water-rinsed plates. Brown a generous pat of butter in a frying pan, and when it "goes quiet" place the meatballs in the pan and let them brown on all sides. Shake the frying pan often. Serve with potato purée or boiled potatoes and raw stirred lingonberries.

Ingredients

4–6 servings
500 g (18 oz) ground (minced) beef/pork mixture
250 ml (1¼ cup) milk
75 g (3 oz) white breadcrumbs
1 egg
1 onion
salt, white pepper
ground allspice

Köttbullar

or Swedish meatballs must be prepared, above all, with love. This is why "Mom's meatballs" are a widespread concept in Sweden, and there are many different favorite recipes. Some people feel there should be grated onion in the meatball mixture itself, while others prefer to dice the onion and fry it separately. Some people feel that their meatballs should be served with thick brown gravy, while others prefer it with a thin meat juice. As part of a smörgåsbord buffet, it is better to skip the gravy altogether.

In southern Sweden many people prefer their ground meat with a little more fat, but the further north you go, the less pork you will find in the meatball mixture. However, bread or rusk crumbs allowed to swell in milk are as important as the lingonberries on the side. They give Swedish meatballs their special soft consistency.

Preparation

Make a pancake batter using the egg, flour and milk. Add salt. Peel the potatoes and grate them. Mix in, then fry small patties of the potato pancake batter in butter until golden brown on both sides. Fry the pork until crunchy. Serve with raw stirred lingonberries.

Ingredients

4–6 servings
1 egg
90 g (3¼ oz) wheat flour
300 ml (1½ cup) milk
2 tsp salt
800 g (28 oz) potatoes
50 g (2 oz) butter
400–500 g (14–18 oz) salt pork
raw stirred lingonberries

Raggmunk

is the name for a Swedish potato pancake. The pancakes are fried in butter and served with fried pork and lingonberries. They cannot be made using new potatoes, since potatoes that are harvested in early summer do not contain enough starch to hold the pancake together. On the other hand, this dish is typical hearty winter fare, so it doesn't matter.

The more crispy and buttery the pancake is around the edges, the better it tastes. The trick is not to spread the batter too thickly. And if you mix a little diced onion into the recipe, this Swedish potato pancake can also be called "French."

Preparation

Peel and boil the potatoes. Mash them and mix with the egg yolks and salt. Let the purée cool, then mix in the flour. Knead the dough thoroughly and shape into a roll. Chop the pork into small cubes and dice the onion. Fry the pork quickly with the onion and mix with the allspice. Cut the potato roll into inch-thick slices, make a depression in the center of each slice and fill it with the pork mixture. Flatten each dumpling so the pork mixture is in the middle and roll into a smooth, even ball. Boil the dumplings slowly in a pot of lightly salted water without a lid for 5–6 minutes after the dumplings rise to the surface. Serve with lingonberries and melted butter. The dumplings can also be cut in half and fried in butter.

Ingredients

4–6 servings
10 medium-sized potatoes
2–3 egg yolks
150–180 g (5–6½ oz) wheat flour
1 tsp salt
1 onion
200 g (7 oz) salt pork
2 tsp cracked allspice

Kroppkakor

is Swedish for filled potato dumplings. Potatoes have been the staff of life in Sweden during the past few centuries. Despite a variety of local names, potato dumplings are eaten throughout the country.

There are many recipes for filled potato dumplings. Actually the only thing they have in common is that they are boiled in water. The other details are open to constant discussion, depending on what local tradition offers: Barley flour or wheat flour? Boiled or raw potatoes? Pork and onion filling or mushroom filling? Eaten with melted butter? Lingonberries? Mustard?

Preparation

Finely chop the onion and cut the beets into small cubes. Mix the ground beef with the egg yolks, a little water, plus salt and pepper into a smooth batter. Add onion, capers and beets plus a little of the beet juice. Shape into small round patties. Place a pat of butter in a frying pan and quickly fry the beef patties on both sides, without letting them become well done inside.

Ingredients

4–6 servings
500 g (18 oz) ground (minced) beef
100–200 ml (½–1 cup) water
3 egg yolks
½ onion
150 g (5 oz) pickled beets + juice
35 g (1¼ oz) capers
salt, white pepper

Biff à la Lindström

is a Swedish classic with a Russian connection. Resembling a hamburger but with the sweet taste of beets and the saltiness of capers, it was introduced in Sweden in 1862 by Henrik Lindström, who had been born and raised in a Swedish family in St. Petersburg. Lindström instructed the kitchen on how to make his special fried beef patty while visiting a hotel restaurant in the southeastern Swedish city of Kalmar. From there, the recipe spread all over Sweden.

In miniature format, this beet-packed patty is a delicacy that is part of the classic Swedish smörgåsbord, so today it is fair to say that beef à la Lindström is eaten all over the world.

Chop up the bones and roast them along with any gristle and tendons in a hot oven. Peel the carrot and celery, cut all vegetables in centimeter (½ in) sized pieces (leave the outside on the onion). Brown the vegetables in a little oil in a spacious, thick-bottomed pot. Add bones and pour red wine and water over until covered. Allow to boil and skim the top thoroughly the whole time. Add spices and garlic cloves (divided). Let simmer slowly for at least one hour. Strain the gravy, then boil down until about 500 ml (2½ cups) remain.

Peel the potatoes and boil them until soft. Press through a ricer and add warm milk and butter. Add salt and pepper to taste.

Cut off the bread crusts and use a food processor to make bread crumbs. Sprinkle half the bread crumbs on a wax paper and save the rest. Grind the wild game ground meat a second time in a meat grinder. Place the ground meat in a food processor, add salt, freshly ground white pepper and egg yolks. Turn on the food processor and pour in the cream. Shape six large flat ground meat patties and place on the wax paper. Sprinkle the rest of the bread crumbs on top. Fry the patties in a frying pan with a little butter, turn them over and place in an oven (175°C/350°F) for 6–8 minutes. Finely chop the shallot and brown in a little butter along with the peas. Add salt and freshly ground white pepper to taste. Place the Wallenbergers on a plate along with peas and mashed potatoes. Beat the gravy with a pat of butter and taste. Garnish the plate with browned wild mushrooms if desired. Pour the gravy around the edges.

6 servings
wild game bones
1 carrot
1 piece of celery root
1 leek
2 onions
2 tbs canola or sunflower oil
1 bottle of red wine
3 garlic cloves
10 white peppercorns
2 bay leaves
3 cloves, 6 juniper berries
700–800 g (25–28 oz) potatoes
300 ml (1½ cup) milk
50 g (2 oz) butter
2–3 slices white bread
600 g (21 oz) wild game ground (minced) meat
5 egg yolks
500 ml (2½ cups) heavy whipping cream
butter for frying
1 shallot
300 g (10 oz) frozen peas
salt, white pepper
wild mushrooms

Viltwallenbergare

or wild game Wallenbergers are a tribute to the generous supply of game in the vast Swedish forest. Moose, roe deer, stag, hare and fowl … Those who travel some distance from major cities will soon find plenty of ordinary people whose freezers are full of wild game. The name Wallenberger comes from the Wallenberg family, a prominent Swedish financial and industrial dynasty. This rich creamy ground meat patty is otherwise usually made with veal.

Preparation

Cut about 12 slices from some small mushrooms and save for the garnish. Finely chop the shallots, and sauté them in a pat of butter without browning. Chop the rest of the mushrooms into pieces, add them to the onions and pour on the chicken bouillon. Simmer for about 10 minutes. Then pour everything into a blender. After blending, pour the soup through a strainer and back into a saucepan. Add the cream, and cook for another few minutes. Salt and pepper to taste. Finely chop the parsley. Fry the saved mushroom slices quickly in a little butter in a hot frying pan. Pour the soup into warm bowls, place the mushroom slices on top and sprinkle with a little parsley.

Ingredients

4 servings
2 shallots
400 g (14 oz) porcini mushrooms
300-500 ml (1½-2½ cups) chicken bouillon
200-400 ml (1-2 cup) heavy whipping cream
3 sprigs of parsley
50 g (2 oz) butter
salt, white pepper

Svampsoppa

or mushroom soup is frankly less common on Swedish tables than mushroom gravy, mushroom omelets, creamed mushroom, mushroom in stews … But it is quite true that Swedes both pick and eat wild mushrooms. After a suitably warm and humid summer, the country's forests are bulging with edible mushrooms, and the handsome Karl Johan (porcini) mushroom grows in such ample quantities that Sweden even exports it.

As summer draws to a close, it is a source of pleasure for people throughout the country to go out hunting for chanterelles. And if they don't find any mushrooms left in the forest, they can go to the outdoor market, where they are always available.

KLARGRAVAD STRÖMMING

Preparation

To make this twice-marinated Baltic herring dish, remove the skin from the filets and place them in the first marinade of water, vinegar and salt for 4–5 hours. Take out the fish and drain the marinade off. Mix the ingredients for marinade 2 and pour it over the Baltic herring filets. Place in the refrigerator overnight. Sprinkle finely chopped chives on top before serving.

Ingredients

4–6 servings
1 kg (2¼ lb) Baltic herring filets
1 bunch of chives
Marinade 1:
500 ml (2½ cups) water
100 ml (½ cup) distilled white vinegar (12%)
1 tbs salt
Marinade 2:
500 ml (2½ cups) water
85 g (3¼ oz) sugar
100 ml (½ cup) distilled white vinegar (12%)
10 crushed white peppercorns
50 ml (¼ cup) oil (not olive oil)

INLAGD SILL

Preparation

To make this marinated herring dish, mix water, vinegar and sugar, boil for a few minutes in a saucepan and let the marinade cool. Cut the presoaked filets into pieces 2 cm (¾ in) wide, peel and slice the onion, and crush the allspice. Alternate pieces of herring with onion inside a jar, insert the bay leaf and pour the marinade on top. Refrigerate for at least 24 hours, preferably for a week.

Ingredients

4–6 servings
4 presoaked herring filets
150 ml (¾ cup) water
5 tbs distilled white vinegar (12%)
85 g (3¼ oz) sugar
1 red onion
10 whole allspice
1 bay leaf

Silltallrik

or a "herring plate" may be viewed as a miniature variation of the more grandiose Swedish "herring table." Fatty herring from the North Sea is a fundamental part of the Swedish diet. When herring were caught, they provided food for many people. To make sure that the herring would last a long time, they were preserved by salting while still raw.

Presoaked vinegar-marinated herring filets may assume many shapes. Herring with onions (löksill), with spices (kryddsill) and with mustard (senapssill) are classics, but in recent years it has become equally popular to flavor the herring with garlic, for example. The accessories are simple, because the herring is the obvious star of the show. Those who wish may add such flourishes as a piece of well-aged cheese, a little sour cream, a slice of crispbread and/or a few freshly boiled potatoes.

Preparation

Cut off the crusts of the bread slices. Sauté the bread golden brown on both sides in a little butter. Place on paper towels. If the shrimps are large, cut them into smaller pieces. Save four sprigs of dill for garnishes. Finely chop the rest of the dill and mix with the shrimps, mayonnaise and mustard. Apportion the mixture on the slices of sautéd bread. Shape the whitefish roe like eggs and place on top of each toast. Garnish each with a sprig of dill and serve with a slice of lemon.

Ingredients

4 servings
4 slices of white bread
320 g (11 oz) peeled shrimps (prawns)
4 tbs mayonnaise
1 tbs Dijon mustard
150 g (5 oz) whitefish roe
50 g (2 oz) fresh dill
1 lemon
butter

Toast Skagen

is an elegant combination of shrimp and other ingredients on a small piece of sautéd bread. It was created by the popular Swedish restaurateur Tore Wretman. More than anyone else, he embraced Swedish culinary traditions during the decades immediately after World War II. At a time when home cooking was starting to fade away and be replaced by foreign fast food, he also elevated classic Swedish dishes into fancy restaurant repertoire, lending them new status.

Named for a fishing port at the northern tip of Denmark, in Sweden toast Skagen is an appetizer that means "party." People who really want to celebrate something are extravagantly generous with the whitefish roe. The sprig of dill on the top serves as a fanfare.

Preparation

Scale the salmon and remove the small bones, but leave the skin on. Make a few cuts in the skin so the marinade will penetrate from below. Mix salt, sugar, pepper and sprinkle it beneath and on top of the salmon filet along with plenty of dill. Place a weighted cutting board on top of the salmon filet and let it marinate at room temperature for 2–4 hours. Then refrigerate for 24–48 hours, turning the salmon filet a few times. Rinse the salmon in cold water. Cut into thin slices without getting too close to the skin, so the dark salmon is included.

Gravlax sauce is served alongside the dill-cured salmon. Mix the mustard, sugar and vinegar and season with salt and fresh-ground pepper. Stir vigorously, while pouring on the oil in a steady, thin stream. When the sauce has attained a mayonnaise-like consistency, stir in the chopped dill.

Ingredients

6 servings
750 g (26 oz) fresh salmon filet with skin on
85 g (3¼ oz) sugar
120 g (4 oz) salt
8 tbs chopped dill
1 tsp crushed white pepper

Sauce:
2 tbs mild Swedish mustard
1 tsp Dijon mustard
2 tbs sugar
1½ tbs red wine vinegar
salt, white pepper
200 ml (1 cup) oil (not olive oil)
chopped dill

Gravad lax

or dill-cured salmon should preferably be served with a mustard sauce, which is French in origin. This marinated salmon dish, along with marinated herring, used to awaken suspicion among tourists. Eat raw fish? Can that be good for you? Nowadays dill-cured salmon is a popular delicacy in the English-speaking world too, and English has simply adopted the short version of its name, gravlax, along with the dill-fragrant, sugar- and salt-marinated fish itself.

Dill-cured salmon is always featured in the Swedish smörgåsbord, but to experience its fine flavor to the full, enjoy a few thin slices of gravlax unaccompanied by other dishes. It is perfect as an appetizer (starter) as well.

Preparation

Place the Baltic herring filets skin side down on a cutting board or similar surface. Salt them and give them a few turns from the white pepper mill, then put together the filets in pairs. Roll the filets in coarse rye flour and fry them in butter until golden brown on both sides. Eat them right away with potatoes and lingonberries, as in the photo, or make a marinated version as follows.

Marinated fried Baltic herring:
Mix all the marinade ingredients and boil for a few minutes in a pot. Place the finished fried Baltic herring filets, while still warm, on top of each other in a deep bowl or dish. Pour the warm marinade over them. Let stand until cool. Peel the red onion, divide it in two, slice it thin and sprinkle on top.

Ingredients

4–6 servings
1 kg (2¼ lb) Baltic herring filet
coarse rye flour
salt, white pepper
butter

Marinade:
350 g (12 oz) sugar
300 ml (1½ cup) distilled white vinegar (12%)
600 ml (3 cups) water
2 tbs whole allspice
2–4 bay leaves
2 red onions

Stekt strömming

or fried Baltic herring is one of hundreds of recipes based on the smaller-sized eastern relative of the North Sea herring. Swedes often say that Baltic herring is better the fatter it is, but the truth is perhaps that all Baltic herring tastes good. Some people prefer to fry the filets laid together with parsley between them. Others want the backbone to stay in. But no one talks about frying Baltic herring in anything but butter.

Freshly fried Baltic herring tastes especially good on top of buttered hard crispbread. But there is certainly nothing wrong about eating them with fluffy mashed potatoes generously sprinkled with chopped parsley.

Preparation

Boil the potatoes, and peel them once they have cooled. If desired, presoak the slices of salmon in milk or water for a few hours to draw out the salt. Peel and slice the onion. Sauté it in a little butter until it softens, without browning. Grease an ovenproof baking dish, cover the bottom with potato slices, spreading half the onions on top and then half the salmon and chopped dill. Cover with a new layer of potato slices, then the rest of the onion, salmon and dill. Finish with a layer of potato slices. Beat together milk, cream and eggs plus salt and pepper. Pour this mixture on top of the salmon pudding and finish with a few pats of butter. Bake in oven (200°C/400°F) for 45–60 minutes, or until the pudding feels firm. Serve with melted butter.

Ingredients

4–6 servings
400 g (14 oz) salt-cured salmon
1½ kg (3¼ lb) unpeeled potatoes
4 eggs
300 ml (1½ cup) heavy whipping cream
300 ml (1½ cup) milk
2 onions
1 large bunch of dill
salt, white pepper

Laxpudding

or salmon pudding is based on the traditional Swedish housewife's firm conviction that a good dinner provides an excellent basis for the next day's lunch. With a little salmon, a little cream and a few potatoes, you can go a very long way. As usual in home cooking, it is possible to vary the ingredients, provided you adjust the amount of salt. Thus the salmon in the pudding may be boiled, smoked or salt-cured, since the basic rule is always that "you take what you have at home." The main thing is to make sure that the result is delicious.

Salmon pudding is traditionally eaten with melted butter. A little fresh lemon juice is a tasty alternative.

Preparation

Peel the potatoes and cut them into strips. Peel and cut the onions into thin slices, sautéing them gently in a little butter without browning. Grease an ovenproof baking dish and cover the bottom with a layer of potatoes, then add half the onions and half the sprat ("anchovy") filets. Another layer of potatoes, then the rest of the onion and sprats. Finish with a layer of potatoes. Flatten the surface, apply a few turns of pepper fresh from the mill and sprinkle on a little salt. Pour the cream on until it is almost visible through the potatoes. Place a few pats of butter on top and, if desired, sprinkle with some breadcrumbs. Bake in the oven (250°C/475°F) for about an hour.

Ingredients

6–8 servings
1.2 kg (2½ lb) potatoes
400 g (14 oz) onions
375 g (13 oz) spice-cured sprat filets
600 ml (3 cups) heavy whipping cream
salt, white pepper
breadcrumbs
butter

Janssons frestelse

or Jansson's temptation – a creamy potato and anchovy gratin – is said to have been named for Pelle Janzon, a food-loving Swedish opera singer of the early 20th century. In any case, the recipe was published for the first time in 1940, and this rich dish quickly became a classic of the Swedish Christmas dinner table. But Jansson's temptation can just as easily be eaten at any time of year. It is quite remarkable that something as simple as potatoes, onions, anchovies and cream can taste so heavenly.

Preparation

Hard boil the eggs, remove the shells and chop them up. Place in a bowl together with the egg yolks and Kalles Kaviar (creamed, smoked cod roe with oil, which comes in a tube). Mix them together. Chop the sprat ("anchovy") filets and blend in. Cut the dill and chives very finely, and chop the parsley. Mix everything together and serve cold, shaped like a small steak tartare and preferably on a slice of kavring, a coarse dark rye bread.

Ingredients

4–6 servings
6 eggs
2 egg yolks
2–3 tbs Kalles Kaviar
125 g (4 oz) spice-cured sprat filets
1 small bunch of parsley
1 small bunch of dill
1 bunch of chives

Gubbröra

is an egg-anchovy salad whose colorful Swedish name means "old man's mix." Swedish culinary tradition includes numerous dishes that are based on seafood or meat that has been salted to last a long time, in this case the spice-cured sprat known in Sweden as "anchovies." Egg-anchovy salad is best served as an appetizer on a thin slice of round dark bread. A small slice of lemon or a sprig of dill on top looks nice. If served as a midnight snack, elegance is not so crucial. The salty taste of the egg-anchovy salad is also suitable at such an hour. Perhaps with a glass of beer?

KAVIARSTRÖMMING

Preparation

Remove the dorsal fin of the Baltic herring and spread the filets with the skin side down. Grease an ovenproof baking dish with butter. Finely chop the dill and make a mixture of Kalles Kaviar (creamed, smoked cod roe with oil, which comes in a tube), egg yolks and dill. Place a teaspoon of the mixture on each Baltic herring filet and roll up each filet beginning from the tail. Place them close together in the baking dish. Whip the cream, blend with the rest of the Kalles Kaviar mixture and spread over the rolled filets. Bake in the oven (220°C/425°F) for about 20 minutes. This dish, whose name means "Baltic herring with caviar," may be served hot or cold.

Ingredients

4–6 servings
1 kg (2¼ lb) Baltic herring filets
150 ml (¾ cup) Kalles Kaviar
3 egg yolks
1 bunch of dill
200 ml (1 cup) heavy whipping cream
butter

KRÄFTSTRÖMMING

Preparation

Remove the dorsal fin of the Baltic herring. Grease an ovenproof baking dish with butter. Sprinkle 1 teaspoon of salt and 1 teaspoon of dill seeds on the bottom of the dish. Roll the Baltic herring filets, skin side in, and place in the baking dish. Pour tomato juice over them and sprinkle the rest of the salt and dill seeds on top. Cover with aluminum foil and bake in the oven (225°C/425°F) for about 20 minutes. Let cool in the baking dish. This dish, whose name means "Baltic herring with crayfish spices," should be served cold.

Ingredients

4–6 servings
1 kg (2¼ lb) Baltic herring filets
2 tsp salt
2 tsp dill seeds (or preferably fresh dill tops in season)
500 ml (2½ cups) tomato juice
butter

ANSJOVISSTRÖMMING

Preparation

Remove the dorsal fin of the Baltic herring and spread the filets with the skin side down. Grease an ovenproof baking dish with butter. Peel and finely chop the onion. Sauté it quickly in a little butter and spread it on the bottom of the baking dish. Divide the sprat ("anchovy") filets the long way, place one on each Baltic herring filet and roll up the herring with the skin facing out, beginning from the tail. Place the filets close together in the baking dish. Pour sprat brine on top, and sprinkle with a little bread crumbs. Finish with a few pats of butter and bake in the oven (220°C/425°F) for about 20 minutes. This dish, whose name means "Baltic herring with anchovies," should be served hot.

Ingredients

4–6 servings
1 kg (2¼ lb) Baltic herring filets
1 onion
125 g (4 oz) spice-cured sprat filets
bread crumbs
butter

Strömmingslådor

are Baltic herring casseroles and they exist in countless variations. Sometimes the Baltic herring filets are rolled with the skin facing outward, sometimes inward. Sometimes the recipe calls for pouring a tomato sauce on top, sometimes dotting the top with butter, sometimes sprinkling with rusk crumbs. Sometimes the filets are spiced with parsley, sometimes with chives, sometimes with sprat filets (commonly known in Sweden as "anchovies"), sometimes with dill. Choose the one you like. They all taste equally good. Or make several dishes if you have guests, and serve a generous "Baltic herring table." Bread, butter, a tasty hard cheese and a generous bowl of freshly boiled potatoes are the only accessories needed.

Preparation

Clean the salmon filets and remove any remaining bones with tweezers. Cut the salmon into six equally large pieces and place them in a baking dish or pan with high edges, about a centimeter (½ in) apart. Sprinkle a little salt over them.

Clean and cut the vegetables into slices. Place all marinade ingredients in a saucepan and boil for 10 minutes. Pour the boiling marinade over the salmon, covering the fish under at least 1 cm (½ in). Then cover the baking dish with plastic film or wax paper and let it stand and slowly cool.

Place an egg yolk, mustard and vinegar plus salt and pepper in a bowl. Beat with an electric egg beater and add the oil in a thin stream while continuing to beat. Then mix the mayonnaise with sour cream or crème fraiche and finely chopped dill. Taste and, if necessary, add more mustard and spices.

Peel the cucumber "sloppily" so a little dark green remains on the outside. Slice it thin, salt it and place in a strainer bowl with a weight on top for an hour or so. Mix a "123 marinade": 1 part vinegar, 2 parts sugar and 3 parts water. Beat until the sugar has dissolved. Sprinkle a few turns of fresh pepper from the mill, add the cucumber and a little chopped parsley.

Serve the salmon with freshly boiled new potatoes.

Ingredients

6–8 servings
1.2 kg (2½ lb) salmon filets with skin

Marinade:
3 liters (3 qt) water
100 ml (½ cup) white wine vinegar
2 tbs salt
5 white peppercorns
5 whole allspice
2 bay leaves
1 onion
1 carrot
½ leek

Dill mayonnaise:
1 egg yolk
1 tbs Dijon mustard
1 tbs good vinegar
salt, white pepper
200 ml (1 cup) canola oil
100 ml (½ cup) sour cream or crème fraiche
1 bunch of dill

Pressed cucumber:
1 cucumber
distilled white vinegar (12%)
sugar
water
parsley

Kall inkokt lax

or cold poached salmon is a Swedish Midsummer classic, served with a dollop of mayonnaise, pressed cucumber and the year's first new potatoes boiled in dill. The traditional dessert is strawberries and whipped cream, perhaps served on top of sponge cake to make an attractive strawberry shortcake.

Salmon in every form – salted, marinated, smoked – is a classic element of the smörgåsbord, and this also applies to the poached cold variety. All forms of salmon also make superb appetizers (starters) or elegant lunches.

Snaps and glögg

means aquavit and hot mulled wine. They are a part of the Swedish culinary tradition. Both those who prefer to skip the aquavit and those who carefully select their favorite one know that this form of vodka is among the pleasures of the Swedish table.

It is traditionally served in a small long-stemmed "snaps glass" of a type which, of course, is made by several of Sweden's famous crystal glassworks.

A glass of *snaps* (sometimes known by the German name *schnapps*) may be large or small, but it is distilled from grain or potatoes and may be spiced in an endless variety of flavors, always taken from nature. Wormwood, caraway, St. John's wort, bog-myrtle and black-currant are typical examples.

In Sweden it is customary to offer guests a snaps when herring is served. Aquavit is also among the usual accompaniments during those late summer parties featuring whole crayfish boiled with dill, as well as at Christmas, when a snaps glass may be decorated with the Swedish equivalent of Santa Claus.

The Swedes often sing traditional drinking songs with their snaps. The most popular one is called "Helan går."

Glögg is a spiced, sugared and simmered (or "mulled") red wine. In Sweden this is a beverage consumed almost exclusively during the Christmas season, usually with raisins and blanched almonds added.

Västerbottenost, svecia and kryddost

are three examples of the Swedish hard cheese tradition. Västerbotten cheese is aged for more than a year and comes from northern Sweden, *svecia* is another aged hard cheese, and *kryddost* is a hard cheese spiced with caraway and sometimes with cloves. The country has many other hard cheeses as well. Back in the days when there were hundreds of Swedish dairies, practically every one of them had its own special hard cheese.

Cheeses that people can cut with a small razor-style cheese slicer are found on practically every Swedish breakfast table. Hotel breakfast buffets usually offer several kinds to choose from. Early in the day, many Swedes prefer a hard cheese with a mild taste, meaning one that has been aged for a shorter period. The later it is during the day, the more they appreciate a cheese with a stronger taste, which has been aged for a longer period.

Aside from snaps, the traditional Swedish herring table includes a well-aged hard cheese, often eaten on crispbread or perhaps a dark rye bread like *kavring*.

Kavring and knäckebröd

are two breads found in virtually every Swedish smörgåsbord. Both are typical of Sweden's traditional food storage culture. *Kavring* is a dense, dark rye bread boasting lots of flavor. *Knäckebröd*, translated as crispbread or hard bread, is usually also baked from rye. The dough is rolled into large pieces, and the bread is dried after baking for the sake of both flavor and shelf life.

Kavring and crispbread are found in many local versions all over Sweden. *Tunnbröd*, a light-colored bread that is rolled very, very thin and is available in both soft and hard varieties, is typical of northern Sweden.

Preparation

Place egg yolks in a bowl, add sugar and beat vigorously over boiling water to a fluffy, sabayon-like consistency. Remove from the heat, continue to beat until cooled and blend in the cloudberry jam (first put through a strainer to remove the seeds) and liqueur. Whip the cream into a foam that is not too hard, then carefully pour onto the egg batter. Divide the parfait into two low, round molds. Place the molds in the freezer for at least 3 hours or until the parfait has become completely hard.

Mix all the dry ingredients for the nut bottoms. Beat the egg whites a little, blending them with the butter and with the dry ingredients into an even batter. Spread out in three circles (equivalent in size to the parfait molds) on a greased baking sheet or baking paper. Bake in the oven (200°C/400°F) to a golden brown color. Take out and remove from the surface before they completely harden.

To make the sauce, beat the egg yolks, sugar and liqueur into a fluffy sabayon over low heat. Remove from the heat and continue to beat until cooled. Whip the cream and carefully add to the sauce.

Place the parfait bottoms between the nut bottoms and sprinkle a little confectioner's sugar on top. Serve with the cloudberry liqueur sauce.

Ingredients

About 10 servings
8 egg yolks
200 ml (1 cup) strained cloudberry jam
100 ml (½ cup) cloudberry liqueur
100 g (3½ oz) sugar
600 ml (3 cups) heavy whipping cream

Nut bottom:
50 g (2 oz) ground hazelnuts
50 g (2 oz) ground blanched almonds
25 g (1 oz) wheat flour
160 g (5 oz) sugar
2 egg whites
50 g (2 oz) melted butter

Sauce:
2 egg yolks
40 g (1½ oz) sugar
50 ml (¼ cup) cloudberry liqueur
200 ml (1 cup) heavy whipping cream

Hjortronparfait

or cloudberry parfait is one of many Swedish desserts based on domestic wild or cultivated berries. Raspberries, blueberries, strawberries, currants and gooseberries are used for jam, juice, compote and jelly, and of course also as flavorings in pies and cakes. It is common to freeze the berries and let them embellish winter desserts. A warm berry sauce on ice cream is incredibly good.

The most frequently used wild berries are lingonberries. They contain a natural preservative, which makes it possible to stir the berries with sugar to make a jam entirely without cooking. Also occupying a place of honor on Swedish tables are golden yellow cloudberries. These berries grow wild in the wetlands of northern Sweden and are a sought-after delicacy.

Preparation

Soak the rose hips in half the water for a few hours. Then boil them soft in the same water. This may take 20–30 minutes depending on their thickness. Blend in a mixer and pass through a sieve. Boil the rest of the water. Stir potato flour into a little cold water. Beat the mixture into the water and boil again. Add the mashed rose hips and sugar. Taste and let cool.

Ingredients

4 servings
100 g (4 oz) dried rose hips
1 liter (1 qt) water
1 tbs potato flour
40 g (1½ oz) sugar

Nyponsoppa

or rose-hip soup is an everyday classic among Swedish desserts. Along with a few macaroons or almond flakes, plus a dollop of whipped cream on top, this soup suddenly turns into party food. Rose hip is very rich in vitamin C and the soup is a gorgeous red in color, making it a pleasure to eat in a country that is too cold and wintry dark much of the year to allow the cultivation of oranges.

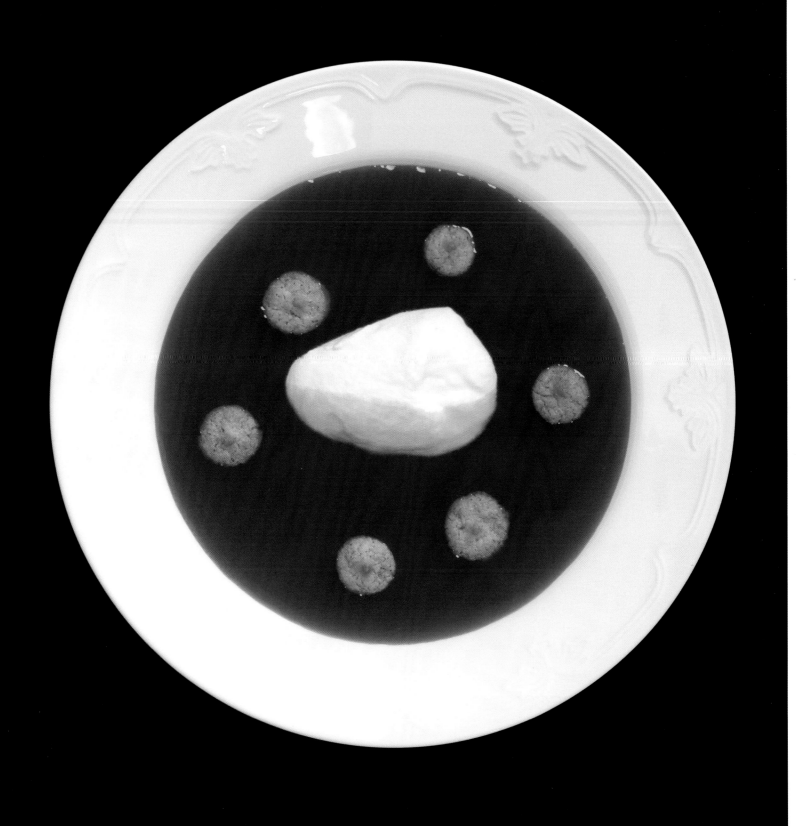

Preparation

Crumble the yeast in a bowl and stir in a few tablespoons of milk. Melt the butter and pour the milk on it. Add the rest of the ingredients and knead the dough in a dough mixer for 10–15 minutes. Let the dough rise while covered at room temperature for 30 minutes.

Roll out the dough so it is about 3 mm (⅛ in) thick and 30 cm (12 in) wide. Spread the room-temperature butter on top. Make a mixture of sugar and cinnamon and sprinkle it over the dough. Roll the dough the long way and cut the roll into about 25 slices. Place them with the cut edge upward in paper molds. Place on a baking sheet and let rise under a towel for about 60 minutes or until the buns have doubled in size.

Beat together the egg and water, brush the mixture carefully on the buns and sprinkle pearl sugar on top. Bake in the oven (220ºC/425ºF) for 5–6 minutes. Allow to cool on a rack.

Ingredients

25 buns
35 g (1¼ oz) yeast
100 g (3½ oz) sugar
300 ml (1½ cup) milk
1 egg
120 g (4 oz) butter
1 tsp salt
1 tbs ground cardemom
750 g (26 oz) wheat flour

Filling:
100 g (4 oz) butter
50 g (2 oz) sugar
2 tbs cinammon

Glaze:
1 egg
2 tbs water
pearl sugar

Kanelbullar

or cinnamon buns are a classic at Swedish coffee parties. During the golden age of home baking, such parties turned into orgies of sweet yeast breads, small cookies, cookies with fillings, pastries and cakes. This tradition lives on in Sweden. If you are invited to someone's home for coffee, you always get a cinnamon bun, a cookie or a piece of cake with it. And at cafés, dainty little cookies continue to compete with all those supersized American muffins.

Preparation

To make gingersnaps, heat the brown sugar, white sugar, corn syrup and water in a pot. Add the butter and let it melt. Stir and let cool slightly, then blend in the spices and baking soda. Then mix in the flour to a smooth consistency. Sprinkle a little flour on top and put the dough out to cool, preferably overnight. Take the dough and knead it smooth on a baking table, adding more flour if desired. Roll it thin and cut into shapes, using the desired cookie cutters. Bake in the oven (180°C/350°F) for 8–10 minutes. Let the gingersnaps cool on the baking sheet.

Ingredients

200 g (7 oz) brown sugar
200 g (7 oz) white sugar
200 g (7 oz) dark corn syrup
150 ml (¾ cup) water
300 g (10 oz) butter
2 tbs ground cinnamon
2 tbs ground ginger
2 tbs ground cloves
1 tbs baking soda
0.9–1 kg (2–2¼ lb) flour

Preparation

To make "Lucia cats" (lussekatter), grind the saffron along with a cube of sugar, using a mortar and pestle. (For those who think ahead: drip a little cognac on top, and let stand a few days.) Crumble the yeast in a bowl and stir in a few tablespoons of milk. Melt the butter and pour on the milk. Add the rest of the ingredients, except the raisins, and knead the dough in a dough mixer for 10 minutes. Carefully mix in most of the raisins, cover the dough and let it rise for 30 minutes at room temperature. Divide the dough into 25 pieces and roll the buns in an oblong shape, about 10 cm (4 in) long. Cover them and let rest for 10 minutes, then roll them twice as long and twist the ends of each bun in opposite directions to form a sort of figure 8. Put one raisin in the middle of each half figure 8. Place on a greased baking sheet and let rise under a towel for about 90 minutes, or until the buns have doubled in size. Bake in the oven (220°C/425°F) for 5 minutes. Beat together the egg and water, brush the mixture on the buns. Allow to cool on the baking sheet.

Ingredients

25 buns
3 g (⅛ oz) saffron threads
50 g (2 oz) yeast
200 g (7 oz) sugar
300 ml (1½ cup) milk
1 egg
150–200 g (5–7 oz) butter
1 tsp salt
750 g (26 oz) wheat flour
100 g (3½ oz) raisins

Glaze:
1 egg
2 tbs water

Saffransbullar and pepparkakor

means saffron buns and gingersnaps. These are among the traditional Swedish Christmas treats. The sweet yeast rolls that are served during the Christmas season are flavored with golden saffron and dark raisins and often shaped into "Lucia cats" (lussekatter). The gingersnaps are customarily cut in the shape of little men and women, pigs or hearts, and are often decorated with frosting. It is not uncommon for children to help build little houses out of gingersnap dough to celebrate Christmas.

Photo: Håkan Elofsson

Carl Jan Granqvist is innkeeper emeritus of Grythyttan Inn (Grythyttans Gästgivaregård) in Bergslagen, a former mining district of central Sweden. He was the initiator of the Department of Restaurant and Culinary Arts (the Restaurant Academy for short), Örebro University. He holds an honorary doctorate in gastronomy and is professor of culinary arts at the University of Stavanger, Norway.

Lena Katarina Swanberg has had a long career as a reporter, but today she is more of an author than a journalist. She has written more than twenty books, several of them dealing with Swedish food.

Mats Hedman is a graphic designer and art director with Swedish and international clients. He also acted as project manager for this booklet.

Pål Allan is one of Sweden's most renowned advertising photographers. He recently won an award for the world's best designed cookbook.

The dishes were prepared at the Nordic House of Culinary Art (Måltidens Hus i Norden), which houses the Restaurant Academy/Örebro University, a worldclass cookbook library, a gastronomic theater and more. The Nordic House of Culinary Art is located in Grythyttan, which has become an important food and culinary center.

The **Swedish Institute (SI)** is a public agency that promotes interest and confidence in Sweden around the world. SI seeks to establish cooperation and lasting relations with other countries through strategic communication and exchange in the fields of culture, education, science and business.

SI works closely with Swedish embassies and consulates around the world.

Sweden.se, the country's official gateway, is a rich source of information that provides a direct insight into contemporary Sweden in many different languages.

Sweden Bookshop has a wide range of books about Sweden and Swedish fiction in over 50 languages. The bookshop can be found at Slottsbacken 10 in central Stockholm and at **www.swedenbookshop.com.**

The Swedish Institute
Box 7434
SE-103 91 Stockholm
Sweden

+46-8-453 78 00
si@si.se
www.si.se and www.sweden.se

Do you have any views on this SI publication? Feel free to contact us at books@si.se.

© 2005 Lena Katarina Swanberg and the Swedish Institute
Coordinator, recipe selection: Carl Jan Granqvist
Texts: Lena Katarina Swanberg
Translation: Victor Kayfetz
Graphic design: Mats Hedman
Food preparation: Joachim Borenius
Pastries: Johan Sörberg
Food photos: Pål Allan
Nature photos: Mira/NordicPhotos and Bildhuset (cover insides), Folio (pp. 14-15, 26-27)
Fonts: Helvetica Neue and Berling
Paper: 130 g and 250 g Artic silk
Printed by: LJ Boktryck AB, Helsingborg, Sweden 2009
ISBN: 978-91-520-0835-5

Some approximate conversions and abbreviations:
g =.gram = 1/1,000 of a kg
1 kg = kilogram = 2.2 pounds (lb)
ml = milliliter = 1/1,000 of a liter
100 ml = ½ cup
1 liter = 1.06 quart (qt)
1 oz = ounce = 1/32 of a quart (qt) = 28.4 grams (g)
1 lb = 16 oz
1 tsp = teaspoon = 0.17 oz = 5 g
1 tbs = tablespoon = 3 teaspoons =½ oz = 14 g
C = degrees Celsius (or Centigrade)
F = degrees Fahrenheit